D1248749

John Bunyan

by HENRI A. TALON

Published for The British Council
and the National Book League
by Longmans, Green & Co.

Two shillings and sixpence net

The author of this study of the work of John Bunyan, master of a manly prose style, and one of the most important figures of the English Puritan movement of the seventeenth century, is Professor of English Literature at the University of Dijon. His contribution to the *Writers and Their Work Series*, notable as being the first from a scholar of another country, is itself a graceful piece of exposition.

Professor Talon's full-length study of *John Bunyan: The Man and His Works* appeared first in Paris in 1948, and in an English translation in 1951. His new essay is written from a somewhat different perspective; his presentation of *Grace Abounding* is slightly modified; his assessment of the *Pilgrim's Progress* also differs from the fuller treatment in his book, and he has been able to take into consideration articles and studies which have appeared since his own important work was issued. Professor Talon is also the author of the only recent appraisal of William Law, published in 1948. His critical surveys have invariably been received on both sides of the Atlantic with the respect and admiration they deserve. To his Bunyan essay he has a Bibliography which, while it differs in some details from the general pattern of the series, is among the most valuable we have published.

Bibliographical Series
of Supplements to 'British Book News'
on Writers and Their Work

★

GENERAL EDITOR
Bonamy Dobrée

¶ JOHN BUNYAN was born at Elstow, Bedfordshire, probably in November 1628: he died on 21 August 1688 in London and was buried in Bunhill Fields, Finsbury.

BUNYAN

from a drawing by ROBERT WHITE *in the British Museum*

JOHN
BUNYAN

by

HENRI A. TALON

PUBLISHED FOR
THE BRITISH COUNCIL
AND THE NATIONAL BOOK LEAGUE
BY LONGMANS, GREEN & CO.

828
B942Yt

99410

LONGMANS, GREEN AND CO. LTD.
48 Grosvenor Street, London, W.1

Associated companies, branches and representatives
throughout the world

First published 1956
Reprinted with additions to bibliography 1964
Reprinted edition © Henri A. Talon, 1964

Printed in Great Britain by
F. Mildner & Sons, London, E.C.1

Alverno College Library
Milwaukee, Wisconsin

JOHN BUNYAN

I

JOHN BUNYAN, man of the people, village tinker, had no other ambition in his writing than to serve his faith and to help his fellows; he had no idea of producing a masterpiece which would outlast the passage of centuries. Yet today we can hardly imagine the non-existence of *Grace Abounding* and *The Pilgrim's Progress*, so important a place have they won in the English cultural heritage.

Nevertheless, Bunyan has not met with undiluted praise. Though Swift, Johnson, Cowper, Macaulay and many others have rendered him homage, he has had violent detractors. All down the ages, the critical spirit endeavours to find new perspectives and to suggest fresh evaluations; but once an author has become part of history, he is entitled to expect a certain objectivity from his readers, and Bunyan seems to have reached the point where he may enjoy this privilege. One can have more or less liking for him, read him for pleasure or merely as a duty, but his name cannot be ignored.

He owes his position primarily to his talent as a writer, but some of his fame is also due to the virile personality which made him share intensely the fervour of his time, and even to the very lowliness of his social status: Bunyan speaks with the voice of the seventeenth-century working man; his work is the expression of popular culture. And because he combines dramatic genius with a vigorous faith, he helps us more than any other writer to understand Puritanism both as an intellectual movement and as a way of life.

Bunyan was born in the pretty village of Elstow, near Bedford, in 1628, probably in November, as he was baptized on the thirtieth of that month.

In his will his father described himself as a 'braseyer', and his grandfather as a 'pettie chapman'. They were humble folk but of old stock: for three hundred years Bunyans had owned land in Bedfordshire, and in better days they had been yeoman farmers. The family seems to have been degenerating when John brought it fresh vigour.

In spite of the humble circumstances of his parents, 'it pleased God', John says, 'to put it into their hearts to put me to school'. Whether he attended school at Elstow, or Bedford, or Houghton Conquest, a neighbouring parish which boasted a grammar school, Bunyan can only have received a rudimentary education which was soon forgotten, if we are to believe his own words. In the workman's cottage bread-eaters must soon become bread-winners, and John must certainly have begun his apprenticeship to his father's craft at a very early age. But in his autobiography, *Grace Abounding*, he is sparing of details about the first nineteen years of his life, and he does little to satisfy the modern reader's curiosity about those decisive influences which are received in childhood.

His father, Thomas Bunyan, belonged to the Established Church, but he does not seem to have been a deeply religious man or to have possessed great delicacy of feeling. In June 1644 he lost his second wife, in July he lost a daughter; and yet he remarried in August. It is not unlikely that his father's unseemly haste wounded John's over-sensitive nature, and that he was not displeased to be called to arms in the autumn of the same year.

In the war between King and Parliament, Bedfordshire had taken sides with the latter, and John was sent to Newport Pagnell in accordance with a parliamentary edict demanding 225 recruits from the town of Bedford. The garrison was commanded by Sir Samuel Luke, a figure immortalized by Samuel Butler in his amusing though unfair satire, *Hudibras*.

Though Bunyan could have regained his freedom in 1645, he preferred to join another regiment, which was destined for Ireland. What lay behind his choice? A taste for adventure? The desire to fight and to see fresh horizons? We do not know, but whatever John's hopes may have been, they were disappointed. He did not reach Ireland, he never saw active service, and in July 1647 he was back in civilian life.

Twenty-one months in the army at an age when one is so impressionable, so full of ardour and of dreams, could only strengthen the influences of Bunyan's early life; for in those days religious fervour was in the very air men breathed. In his book *Cromwell's Army*, Sir Charles Firth has shown how the army abounded with visionaries; every leader, almost every soldier, was also a preacher and a theologian; and battles opened and closed with prayer.

So at Newport Pagnell as at Elstow, Bunyan lived in a Puritan atmosphere. But what is Puritanism? Broadly speaking, it is an austere disciplining of life in the service of a fervid religious faith. It has been asserted that the Bible constituted the whole of religion for the Protestants, and certainly its authority was accepted by the Puritans with the utmost rigour. Bunyan speaks for almost all Puritans when he writes, with reference to the Scriptures, 'all our words are truth, one of as much force as another'. For them the Bible is 'school of all wisdom, sole food of our spirits', as Calvin says; it is all knowledge, according to Bunyan; it is a model for government, according to Thomas Cartwright, Lady Margaret Professor of Divinity at Cambridge, who in 1571 gave so great an impetus to Puritanism.

But the doctrine which is at the heart of Puritanism, without which one can understand nothing of Bunyan's spiritual torments, is that of election. Neither good works nor holiness of life can save a man, but only faith, the grace of God freely given to the few who are chosen. Hence the restlessness of the Puritan, his habit of introspection, and his intense spiritual life.

The stern exigencies of such a creed could not fail to leave their mark upon private and public life, and Macaulay went so far as to say that Puritanism 'threw over all life a more than monastic gloom'. But the great historian left out of account the depths of gloom which shrouded some of the mediaeval monasteries, and he gave altogether too sombre a picture of Puritan England. Under Cromwell, people did not stop laughing or singing or even dancing. Even without wider

historical investigation, the reading of *The Pilgrim's Progress*
would be enough to give a truer idea of the atmosphere of
the time, and of the kind of spiritual nourishment Bunyan
received in the army and in the village to which he returned
in 1647.

He married soon after his return, perhaps during the
following year, but the exact date is unknown. There is no
mention of the marriage in the registers at Elstow, and no
precise information is given in *Grace Abounding*. Though he
describes carefully his spiritual life and the variations of light
and shade that played upon his consciousness, in his autobiography his marriage is barely mentioned; for, occasionally,
Bunyan shows little understanding of external influence.

Yet his young wife brought him more than the feminine
tenderness of which his mother's death had all too soon
deprived him, more than the two books which were to make
a profound impression upon him: Arthur Dent's *The Plaine
Mans Path-Way to Heaven*, and Lewis Bayly's *The Practice of
Piety;* her greatest gift was the example of her own piety.
Bunyan's marriage ushered in the true spring-time of his
spiritual life. The seeds sown ever since childhood burst forth,
and that painful process began which was to transform the
restless youth into a strong man who had won the mastery of
his soul.

This growth, which Bunyan calls his conversion, cannot
be summarized; it must be read entire in *Grace Abounding*.
Here it only need be said that Bunyan began to frequent the
village church, to read the Bible feverishly, and to give up
innocent amusements which seemed to him sinful. Torn by
doubts and remorse, he went through a period of storm and
stress which was not immediately ended by his joining the
Baptist Church at Bedford in 1653. But membership of a
group where his talents as a preacher were called upon
helped Bunyan to regain his balance and to reflect the
radiancy of the peace he had won.

In 1660 his faith was put to the test by the return of the
Stuarts, who were the enemies of Puritanism. He was arrested

on 10 November 1660. He might have regained his physical liberty at the price of spiritual servitude: if he gave up preaching, he was told, he would be allowed to go back to his family. But Bunyan was not the man to do this. He knew that actions speak louder than words:

Besides, I thought, that seeing God of his mercy should choose me to go upon the forlorn hope in this country, that is, to be the first that should be opposed, for the Gospel; if I should fly, it might be a discouragement to the whole body that might follow after.

And again,

I was not altogether without hopes but that my imprisonment might be an awakening to the saints in the Country.

So he chose prison; and he remained there for twelve years.

It must be stressed that Bunyan did not embrace this sacrifice out of that yearning for martyrdom which is perhaps the subtlest form of pride; he resolved to let himself be thrown into the County Jail at Bedford because he could not do otherwise without betraying both his faith and his brethren. But for one so full of warm human tenderness the choice was not easy:

I found myself a man, and compassed with infirmities. The parting with my wife and poor children hath often been to me in this place as the pulling the flesh from my bones; and that not only because I am somewhat too fond of these great Mercies, but also because I should have often brought to my mind the many hardships, miseries and wants that my poor family was like to meet with, should I be taken from them, especially my poor blind child, who lay nearer my heart than all I had besides.

At the very moment when he was risking his life, he was assailed again by the classic doubt of the Calvinist: am I really among the elect? Will death bring me eternal bliss or eternal torment? This, the crucial moment of his existence, culminated in that decision to venture all for his faith which was for him like a leap in the dark:

Wherefore, thought I, the point being thus, I am for going on, venturing my eternal state with Christ, whether I have comfort here or no. If God doth come in, thought I, I will leap off the ladder even blindfold into eternity, sink or swim, come Heaven, come Hell. Lord Jesus, if Thou wilt catch me, do; if not, I will venture for thy name.

But this courageous gesture enabled him to accomplish one of the tasks which, according to him, God has entrusted to man: 'To find what we are.' His supreme act of will was the supreme revelation of himself to himself. And if, as Ben Jonson, Milton, and many others have thought, it is the high moral quality and the virility of a man which give distinction to his writing, the most creative experience in Bunyan's life was his imprisonment and total renunciation.

In jail he was by no means idle, 'making many hundred grosse of long-tagged thread laces' to keep his family, teaching his fellow-prisoners, giving guidance to those who came to him for advice, and continuing the writing he had begun as far back as 1656, during a controversy with the Quakers.

Of the sixty works which Bunyan has left, fifty-six are now almost forgotten. These pamphlets, sermons, and treatises contain forceful and lively pages, but they belong to old quarrels, and the theology which they express has become foreign to most of us. Anyone interested in the seventeenth century can still find useful material in *The Life and Death of Mr. Badman* (1680); the student of English literature cannot dispense with reading *The Pilgrim's Progress* (1678), a work fraught with spiritual significance; but it must be acknowledged that today, especially on the Continent, *Grace Abounding* (1666) is read with more interest than any other of Bunyan's works.

The theological drama which is unfolded in *The Pilgrim's Progress* awakens less response among modern readers than the forthright account of a spiritual conflict which is given in the autobiographical work. The former has lost for us some of its meaning and much of its urgency; but the introspective analysis of the latter has a universal quality. Even if our faith is not Bunyan's, we are at once aware of the fervour of his exacting conscience and of his unquiet heart. Our doubts and difficulties may not be his, our hopes may have other goals, our sufferings other springs, but how well we recognize the rhythm of the inner life, those accounts of despair and of joy which Bunyan has evoked with such forceful and yet such subtle truth!

After 1668 Bunyan's imprisonment was much less strict. From time to time he was allowed to attend meetings of his sect, as the *Church Book* bears witness. In January 1672, 'after much seeking God by prayer' his brethren chose him as their minister. In March, Charles II signed his Declaration of Indulgence; in May, Bunyan obtained a licence to preach; and in September the royal pardon was officially granted him.

It was therefore with an increased sense of authority that Bunyan resumed his battle for Christ, preaching in the surrounding villages and even going as far as Reading and London. According to his friend Charles Doe, his success was so great that the Londoners flocked to hear him. And the nickname of Bishop Bunyan given him by his enemies also bears witness to the reputation and influence of the preaching tinker.

However, under the Stuarts the liberty of Dissenters was never sure. In 1673 Charles II was constrained to repeal the Declaration of Indulgence, Parliament refusing to admit, as Macaulay puts it, 'an act so liberal done in a manner so despotic'. And when the King called to office the Earl of Danby, who was hostile to the Puritans—and also, may it be said, to the Roman Catholics—religious persecution began again.

On 4 March 1675 a warrant for arrest was issued against Bunyan, but it is doubtful whether he was actually imprisoned again in the County Jail in that year. Miss Joyce Godber has discovered a bond dated 21 June 1677, in which two Londoners were sureties for the release of Bunyan, and she therefore thinks that he was not imprisoned earlier than December 1676. This surmise is worth noting because, as we shall see, another question depends upon it—that of the date of the composition of *The Pilgrim's Progress*, which appeared in 1678. This book extended Bunyan's reputation over the whole of the British Isles, to the Continent, and even as far as America, and earned for him the title *Anglus egregius*, given him in 1708 by a specialist in religious and mystical literature.

In August 1688 Bunyan was called to Reading to settle a quarrel between a father and son. He went there on horse-back, for he was too manly to take the coach, which, as Mr. David Ogg tells us, was considered a sign of effeminacy in the seventeenth century. As a result of a journey of forty miles in the rain, he caught a chill, and was obliged to take to his bed in a friend's house in London. Worn out by his life of labour, he sank rapidly, and died on the last day of the month.

II

It was in Bedford Jail, in 1666, that Bunyan wrote his spiritual autobiography, with the aim of edifying the brethren from whom he was separated. This type of writing belongs to a strong tradition among Dissenters, though it is stronger among Quakers than Baptists. But Bunyan was obeying an inner urge rather than conforming to a tradition.

Protestantism, particularly in its Puritan form, prompts a man to examine his conscience, and even, as John Henry Newman asserted, to contemplate himself:

I do not mean to say that Christ is not mentioned as the Author of all good, but that stress is laid rather on the believing than on the object of belief, on the comfort and persuasiveness of the doctrine rather than on the doctrine itself. And in this way religion is made to consist in contemplating ourselves, instead of Christ; not simply in looking to Christ, but in *seeing* that we look to Christ.[1]

In the spiritual life of every Christian, and of the Puritan more especially, two movements can be discerned: the first, born of penitence and humiliation before the face of God, turns inwards to examine the self; the second is the contrary

[1] *Lectures on Justification.*

movement, drawing away from introspection towards the contemplation of the goals to be attained. And one of the most important of these is the work of evangelization. *Grace Abounding*, it would seem, was created out of these two movements; in it are to be found their ebb and flow, their currents now rushing ahead, now being checked and losing themselves in eddies and backwaters.

Bunyan's need of unburdening himself is turned into a means of edification, and he derives from it a sober pleasure. To tell his life-story is to deepen his awareness of the richness of his own spiritual drama. As Kierkegaard remarked, if life is lived forwards, it is only understood backwards. So memory is the soul of his work as it is the centre of his thought. And in endeavouring, in one book after another and especially in his autobiography, to convert others, Bunyan never ceases to deepen his own faith.

Grace Abounding offers, firstly, a psychological interest. The book sheds light upon Puritan thought and feeling, and it is a remarkable account of the conversion of a religious spirit tinged with mysticism.

It would be impossible here to enter into the question of Bunyan's sincerity, which I have already treated at length elsewhere. But it must at least be pointed out that the resemblances often noted between *Grace Abounding* and other Puritan autobiographies by no means prove that Bunyan was mechanically conforming to the laws of a literary genre.

True, he does imitate. Nobody today would claim for him a kind of intellectual virginity. But this is a secondary matter in literary creation, though it is of prime importance in the formation of a mind. If the confessions of the 'mechanic preachers' offer certain similarities, it is first and foremost because their authors lived at the same period, in the same environment, and passed through similar experiences. Their works bear a family likeness because they themselves shared the same faith. It is a question of souls imitating souls, not of books imitating books.

But *Grace Abounding* is more than a psychological document: it is a literary masterpiece. Though it is too much to say, with Renan, that 'what one says of oneself is always poetry', yet personal confession does at times become great art. It is enough to recall Rousseau's *Confessions*, Goethe's *Dichtung und Wahrheit*, Newman's *Apologia*, Gide's *Et nunc manet in Te*.

The first quality which marks *Grace Abounding* as a work of art is the creative tension communicated to it by the exceptionally vigorous temperament of the author. The second is a kind of impersonality which, paradoxically, is achieved within the very omnipresence of the author. For Bunyan sees in his own story an example—or, as we should say today, a case—which goes beyond himself and attains a general value. Even as he expresses himself in the personal manner, his personality is being effaced. He is already on the way to that dramatic transposition of his experience which is to be fully realized in *The Pilgrim's Progress*.

A comparison of sections 37 and 38 of his autobiography with sections 53 and 54, where he makes use of the same incident, should make this clear. In the former, we see Bunyan going about his work in the little town of Bedford. It is fine. A few housewives stand talking at their doors. Their remarks reflect their Calvinist faith, and they are radiant with peace and joy. In the later paragraphs, the street in Bedford has disappeared. The scene is laid on a hill, everywhere and nowhere at the same time. The spring sun has become a symbolic sun, splendid and almost divine. The little group of pious women has become a chosen people set apart by their faith from the corrupt, doomed world:

About this time, the state and happiness of these poor people at Bedford was thus, in a *dream*, or *vision*, presented to me. I saw, as if they were on the sunny side of some high mountain, there refreshing themselves with the pleasant beams of the sun, while I was shivering and shrinking in the cold, afflicted with frost, snow, and dark clouds. Methought, also, betwixt me and them, I saw a wall that did compass about this mountain.

Bunyan then describes his attempt to break a way through a breach in the wall, and his joy at having succeeded:

Then was I exceeding glad, and went and sat down in the midst of them, and so was comforted with the light and heat of their sun.

This passage contains a keyword: dream, or vision. Dreams, which were daily fare for Bunyan, allow him here, as later in *The Pilgrim's Progress*, to widen his own horizon, and to absorb without effort the lesson which every artist must learn: that to express oneself, one must know how to efface oneself.

A reflection of Pascal's is applicable to Bunyan's self-portrait: 'a portrait comprises both absence and presence.' It comprises the presence of the particular individual represented; and it comprises absence in so far as it goes beyond this individual and offers an image of human kind.

Bunyan tells the story of his life with tact, without ever raising his voice:

I could also have stepped into a style much higher . . . and could have adorned all things more . . . but I dare not. God did not play in convincing of me; the Devil did not play in tempting of me . . . wherefore I may not play in my relating of them . . .

The familiar style is not sought after or cultivated; it comes naturally to the pen of this man of the people:

Yea, my heart . . . would now continually hang back . . . and was as a clog on the leg of a bird to hinder her from flying.

The vocabulary is rendered expressive by its rustic flavour, and often by a kind of concrete solidity:

This, for that instant, did benumb the sinews of my best delights . . . This sentence stood like a mill post at my back . . . I have found my unbelief to set, as it were, the shoulder to the door to keep him out.

The words Bunyan uses reproduce felicitously the phenomena of automatism and the hallucinations which he experienced:

That sentence fell with weight upon my spirit . . . a voice did suddenly dart from Heaven into my soul . . . bolted upon me.

Whether the sentences grip the thought, or give way to the

flow of feeling, they are always vigorous. At times there is a slight breathlessness, a hesitation, but this is soon followed by an eager springing forward towards those personal events which for Bunyan remained forever marvellous: his visions and the miracles which he believed had been worked upon him.

Frequently there are sentences composed almost entirely of monosyllabic Anglo-Saxon words which seem rather harsh:

Peace now, and before I could go a furlong as full of fear and guilt as ever heart could hold; and this was not only now and then, but my whole seven weeks' experience.

But with Bunyan even awkwardness may become beautiful; the lack of polish, the rugged rhythm, the homeliness of the words and their roughness, succeed in convincing us that the mode of expression is perfectly adapted to the thought and feeling. Bunyan's style is part of himself, and it vibrates with him in his struggles and his ecstasies:

Oh! the mount Sion, the heavenly Jerusalem, the innumerable company of angels, and God the judge of all, and the spirits of just men made perfect, and Jesus, have been sweet unto me in this place. I have seen that there, that I am persuaded I shall never, while in this world, be able to express.

One catches in this passage a note of nostalgia for those invisible realms which Bunyan had contemplated. The final vision in *The Pilgrim's Progress* is anticipated here, and we have a foreshadowing of the closing sentence of that work, with its melancholy restraint:

And after that, they (the angels) shut up the gates: which when I had seen, I wished myself among them.

For Bunyan, as for St. Augustine, this realm is not an object of contemplation, but a home.

Biblical reminiscences mingle with personal recollections to give a grave resonance to the style. Sometimes Bunyan uses an actual biblical quotation in the text, sometimes he merely takes a suggestion from the Bible and his imagination transmutes it.

The imagination which enables Bunyan to give a general value to his own life-story also elevates his style. For style, as Proust said, is not made from a recipe, it is a matter of vision. It is because of its style, and the abiding interest of the experiences it describes, that *Grace Abounding* remains a living work.

III

The first part of *The Pilgrim's Progress* was entered in the Stationers' Register on 22 December 1677; it was licensed in February 1678, and published in London the same year. These, the known facts, are not sufficient to satisfy the curiosity of Bunyan scholars. With that regard for precision which does honour to specialists, even when they are playing with a speculation, they want to know when the book was written.

Internal evidence and the interpretation of the facts may lead to various possibilities.

Two-thirds of the way through the book, the story is needlessly interrupted.[1] 'So I awoke from my dream', says the narrator, as if he were going to end his story. And then he carelessly picks up the thread again and begins a new paragraph: 'And I slept and dreamed again.'

What inference may be drawn from this? John Brown, the great biographer of Bunyan, thought that the book was begun during the author's last imprisonment, broken off on his release (I awoke), and taken up again later (I dreamed again).

But when was Bunyan imprisoned for the second time? We have noted the existence of two documents: a warrant of arrest dated 4 March 1675 and a bond for Bunyan's release dated 21 June 1677. Did he then spend another period,

[1] Mr. James F. Forrest has now convinced me that the break is artistically justifiable. See his interesting article: 'Bunyan's Ignorance and the Flatterer: A Study in the Literary Art of Damnation', *Studies in Philology*, LX, i, January, 1963.

of over two years, in Bedford Jail? According to his friend
Charles Doe, the second period of captivity did not last for
more than six months. It is therefore possible that Bunyan
was not after all imprisoned in 1675; but that having failed
to appear before the Archdeacon's Court in 1676 for non-
attendance at the parish church, he was only then sent to jail.

Mrs. Vera Brittain and Mr. Roger Sharrock conclude from
this that *The Pilgrim's Progress* was begun during the first
term of imprisonment and continued during the second,
four or five years later. I cannot believe this. This vigorous
book, in which one feels the pressure of creative force and
creative joy, and the need to press forward as quickly as possible to the end of the road that lies ahead, could not possibly
have been laid aside for four years.

In the verse apology which serves as a preface to *The
Pilgrim's Progress*, Bunyan tells us that the subject came to
him suddenly, while he was writing another book (probably
The Heavenly Footman), which he at once abandoned in
order to follow this new inspiration. Ideas came to him

> Like sparks that from the coals of fire do fly.

Writing had never seemed to him so sweet:

> Thus I set pen to paper with delight.

If, as has been said, works of art can be divided into two
groups, those which are 'obtained' and those which are
'given', *The Pilgrim's Progress* must surely be placed in the
second group.

Some timorous friends objected that the reader would find
in this book only a pleasant tale and be content to enjoy the
'outside' of Bunyan's dream, without seeking its meaning.
Bunyan took no notice of them:

> I print it will; and so the case decided.[1]

---

[1] See Bunyan, *The Author's Apology*, lines 39-49. It is Bunyan's answer
to his friends:
> 'Since you are thus divided
> I print it will; and so the case decided.'
'it', of course, is *The Pilgrim's Progress*.

To our delight, in his haste he even forgot to re-read what he had written. In the first edition the grammar is faulty, but this gives the language all the more relish. Later Bunyan corrected his text, and in 1679 he published a third edition which was revised and considerably expanded.

The allegory had scarcely appeared before the author was being accused of plagiarism:

> Some say the Pilgrim's Progress is not mine.

Modern scholars, given to making finer distinctions, speak only of influences. Since the middle ages, the spiritual life of man had often been likened to a pilgrimage or a battle; there are recurring images which suggest themselves naturally to Christians brought up on the Bible; they are common property. Originality consists, in part, in the art of using the ideas of others and of appropriating anything that may be turned to good account, wherever it may be found.

Bunyan can hardly have failed to know some of his forerunners. If he had not read Guillaume Deguileville's *Le Pélerinage de l'homme*, even though there was a seventeenth-century English version, he had probably come across other allegorical tales inspired by the work of Deguileville. It is certain that he had made use of Richard Bernard's *The Isle of Man*. Bernard has provided him with actual suggestions for one of his books, *The Holy War* (1682), and also, in a more diffused and subtle way, Bernard was one of those who encouraged him

> In handling figure, or similitude

and who emboldened him to indulge in 'fancies [that] will stick like burs'.

The Pilgrim's Progress stands at the meeting-point of various currents of religious and popular literature. Bunyan owes much to the literary convention of 'emblems', or a few lines of verse serving as a commentary on a picture. In the seventeenth century, one of the authors of such emblems, Francis Quarles, was called 'the darling of our plebeian

judgements'. Bunyan, true plebeian, had a taste for this concrete poetical form of teaching and he made use of it. He is
also indebted to the books of 'characters' which were very
fashionable in his day; and he confesses to a liking for sermons written 'dialogue wise'. He owes a particularly heavy
debt to Arthur Dent, whose *The Plaine Mans Path-Way to
Heaven*, which Bunyan's first wife made him read, is a masterpiece of this type of literature. Dent's concrete, sinewy
language heralds Bunyan's, which it has certainly helped to
form.

Finally, before his conversion, Bunyan had been a great
reader of stories and romances:

Give me a ballad, a new-book, George on horseback, or Bevis of
Southampton; give me some book that teaches curious arts, that tells of
old fables.

He had of course given up this profane reading, but he had
not forgotten it. As he was writing *The Pilgrim's Progress*,
his memory was flooded with it. So the pious allegory is not
without its giants, its fierce animals and its monsters; and
what glorious fights there are! The spirit of childhood lives
on in the mature man.

No author ever followed the development of his own
stories with greater interest than Bunyan. If he assumes an
air of detachment in the narrative, he makes up for this in
the margin. There he barefacedly gives way to his feelings:
'O good riddance', 'O brave talkative', 'Christian snibbeth
his fellow'. But the initial enthusiasm passed and Bunyan
realized that he must appear more serious; so, with charming
hypocrisy, he removed from the second edition the excla-
mations which had added relish to the first.

Recollections of romances mingle therefore with biblical
reminiscences in *The Pilgrim's Progress*. Strange bedfellows
indeed. Yet, on reflection, this union of fiction and Scripture
is not surprising, for the Bible was not for Bunyan only the
authentic record of the word of God, but also a collection of
marvellous adventure-stories.

No more surprising is Bunyan's sturdy denial of any debt towards his predecessors:

> It (the Pilgrim) came from mine own heart, so to my head.
> Manner and matter too was all mine own.

When one has carried memories about since childhood, one honestly forgets that they came from outside; and with the help of a little vanity, it is easy to believe oneself more original than one is.

There is no doubt that Bunyan had carried *The Pilgrim's Progress* about with him for a long time. A reading of the books which preceded his greatest work shows how the allegory slowly formed itself and how it was seeking to be born. Here and there, in the sermons and treatises, one comes across the germs of ideas that are to be developed in *The Pilgrim's Progress*, and there are foreshadowings of some of the characters. If the book was conceived suddenly, bearing its author along with it irresistibly, it was preceded by a long, secret preparation.

And after all, when it is reduced to its elements, the pilgrimage of the chief character, Christian, is the story of a conversion, that is to say of an experience so intensely felt by the author as to be ever present in his heart and mind, so that he could not think or write anything without drawing upon it. Invisible, and yet pervading the work with his presence, Bunyan could claim in good faith, if not without pride: 'Manner and matter too was all mine own.'

Only a prolonged study of the text, which it is not possible to undertake here, could do justice to its rich symbolism. Every specific episode assumes a spiritual value and has moral implications. The more one understands Puritanism, the better one can appreciate the significance this or that detail had for Bunyan and his fellow-believers. But *The Pilgrim's Progress* is not wrapped up in the history of its time like a larva in its cocoon. Like every work of art, it has an autonomous existence, and lives on independently of the life of its author. A work of art, Lascelles Abercrombie once said, does not exist in what it may have meant to someone else, but in what it means to me: that is the only way it can exist.

To read this old book with delight, one must achieve the same freshness of response as before a primitive picture or a mediaeval illumination; one must look at certain scenes through Bunyan's eyes, which have been likened to the child-like eyes of those old artists who dressed the builders of the Tower of Babel in the costume of fifteenth-century Italy. But then, having done this, one must venture to read *The Pilgrim's Progress* in the light of present-day thoughts and cares.

One of the first episodes gives the tone of the whole work. The author, sleeping by a cave, sees in a dream a man clothed in rags, turning his face from his own house, a book in his hand and a great burden upon his back. To everyone's amazement he is preparing to leave his own town, for he knows it to be threatened by the wrath divine. His family and friends refuse to follow him, so he sets out alone.

Who is this man? We are not told. It is 'he', a vague pronoun. His identity is not disclosed until after a swamp has been crossed with great difficulty. Whatever may have been the exact value given it by Bunyan, this detail is full of meaning for us, irrespective of the author's intentions. To escape from the accursed city, to lift oneself out of the anonymity of the common herd, one must struggle without ceasing. In the crowd where everyone behaves like everyone else, nobody really exists. Man is degraded and lost in the indefinite. To be worthy of a distinguishing name, one must be capable of taking difficult decisions, of accepting suffering and conflict.

Before Kingsley, Bunyan offered an example of muscular Christianity. Before Kierkegaard, *The Pilgrim's Progress* teaches that the man who fully exists is a man on the march, stumbling but picking himself up again, always there and always elsewhere, because his gaze is fixed upon far horizons which are for ever extending.

Bunyan would perhaps have been surprised by certain details of this commentary, but surely not by its general lines. For the whole book affirms that the Christian life—and indeed any life—must be the expression of a dynamic will. Through his personal experience, Bunyan knows and demonstrates that spiritual man is not a simple product of natural man, but the result and the reward of a persevering struggle.

Christian's path is strewn with obstacles: a door to be opened, a hill to be climbed, a dark valley to be crossed in the fear of death, and a fair, rank with the corruption of a world hostile to pure hearts, which it imprisons, tortures and slays.

But the road also has its pleasant resting-places: the Palace Beautiful, the Delectable Mountains, the Country of Beulah; these rare moments of repose offer the traveller rather the encouragement of a vision than the sweetness of rest. From the Palace Beautiful the Delectable Mountains can be seen, and from their summit Heaven. In *The Pilgrim's Progress*, as in Browning's *Paracelsus*, the pilgrim's way is continually being shortened by the revelation of future truth.

The success of the book called forth a 'sequel'. But Bunyan did not understand the nature of the popular demand. Instead of continuing *The Pilgrim's Progress*, he produced a companion to the portrait of Christian in the portrait of a damned soul: the pilgrimage towards the celestial city is followed by the race down to hell. In 1680 *The Life and Death of Mr. Badman* appeared. It was not at all the sort of book the public was looking for. This was the signal for the publication by a certain T.S. of *The Second Part of the Pilgrim's Progress* (1682). T.S. was not a common forger, but a pious man even more serious-minded than Bunyan. Far from seeking to pass himself off as the tinker, he was endeavouring to correct the latter's errors. His chief aim was to suppress the laughter raised by the story 'in some vain and frothy minds'.

After receiving this lesson about the wishes of his readers, Bunyan went back to his dream, and, at the beginning of 1684, he published the true continuation of his allegory.

IV

The first part of *The Pilgrim's Progress* described a conversion. It was a solitary journey; Christian's two companions, Faithful and Hopeful, are really only two other aspects of himself. Writing from his own intimate experience, Bunyan showed that on the mystical pilgrimage, 'one cannot possibly have company', as Kierkegaard says.

The second part is not the projection of a personal drama, but a transposition of pastoral experience. Bunyan's human horizon has broadened and lost its hardness of line. The author has learnt that one can be a good Christian without having a heroic soul, and that among the elect there are weak people like Mr. Fearing, Mr. Ready-to-Halt, Mr. Much-Afraid, Mr. Feeble-mind.

So the progress of a group is substituted for that of a solitary man. After the grandeur of lone battles comes the warmth of fighting shoulder to shoulder, and the sweetness of friendship.

The doctrinal responsibility of the pastor is shown in details which interested the first readers. As for the presence of women, it can be explained, as Mr. Sharrock says, by the growing place they occupied in the church at Bedford.

As in the first part, the atmosphere is created from the outset, and its quality is sustained throughout. Christian's wife and her friend Mercy set out one 'sunshine morning'. Bunyan has learnt that, as another Puritan, Richard Baxter, says, the signs of a soul reborn are not sorrowing and tears, but love and joy. His dealings with others have taught him this, and also, and above all, his personal experience, which is not recorded completely in *Grace Abounding*. To say, as has sometimes been said, that Bunyan's religion is that of a sick soul, is to ignore the second part of *The Pilgrim's Progress*. On the contrary, his religion is that of a healthy mind.

Christiana's route is the same as her husband's, but where for him darkness brooded, for her there is light. In the journey of the soul throughout the world, it is not the places which change, but the traveller.

Christiana is accompanied by friends whereas Christian journeyed alone, so introspection gives way to the observation of others by a man who smiles at life and allows himself innocent mischief. The tense swift-moving spiritual drama is succeeded by a sort of middle-class novel. Above all, a less narrow ideal of life is manifested, a friendliness towards the good things of the earth, a compassion and a love for mankind which are Bunyan's finest moral and religious message.

A book so richly nourished by self-knowledge and knowledge of others could be no ordinary allegory. Usually, allegory only dresses up phantoms duly labelled Avarice, Lust, Faith, Charity, etc. To every action and every character is attached a precise meaning and one meaning only, which is guessed once and for all. Allegory belongs to the realm of convention. But *The Pilgrim's Progress* belongs to the realm of nature and of life; its pilgrims are not deprived of flesh and blood. Bunyan has even stressed this concrete quality through one of his heroes: 'Not *Honesty* in the abstract, but Honest is my name.'

We are not asked to watch capital-letter Vices and Virtues, but, as Coleridge so aptly put it, villagers whose neighbours have given them nicknames. This is another way of saying that one of the first merits of the book is its realism, its two-fold realism: the psychological realism of the characters, and the descriptive realism of the setting, which owes much to Bedfordshire.

The mystic path of the pilgrims is also an old Roman way, in poor repair, passing by dangerous swamps, resounding to the wheels of coaches, frequented by thieves as well as by honest folk, skirting an orchard enclosed by high walls, or a meadow bounded by hedges. Now it climbs a hill, now descends into a valley which echoes with a shepherd's song.

Bunyan's love of nature is expressed with that vigour which he puts into all his feelings and all his actions:

Here he would lie down, embrace the ground and kiss the very flowers that grew in this valley. He would be up every morning by break of day.

He borrows many details from the life of his time, and his Vanity Fair, that microcosm of a corrupt world, resembles the fairs at Elstow, at Stourbridge near Cambridge, or even St. Bartholomew Fair, immortalized by Ben Jonson.

At times the observation is enlivened by a touch of satire, as in the description of the tribunal before which the pilgrims appeared. To depict this scene, a sorry farce showing only a parody of justice, Bunyan had only to remember his own trial or that of many another Puritan.

The historian can even detect in *The Pilgrim's Progress* the reflection of the author's doctrinal and other quarrels, as well as of his pastoral duties. For it must be remembered that to Bunyan's contemporaries this tale was also, and perhaps even primarily, a tract, of which Coleridge could say, 'It is in my conviction, incomparably the best *summa theologiæ evangelicæ* ever produced by a writer not miraculously inspired'; but a theology, may it be noted, upon which Coleridge was too much inclined to exaggerate Luther's influence at the expense of Calvin's.

The modern reader who is unable to discern what is polemic and propaganda and strict Calvinism in the book must lose part of its primary meaning. But our unawareness of some of the original implications of the allegory does not necessarily lead to a weakening of its human significance and its reduction to 'a pleasant narrative of devils and angels', to quote a critic of the historical school. In any case in the second part these angels and devils are almost entirely superseded by familiar figures, grouped together in numerous scenes where the dignity of the Puritan home is charmingly depicted.

Bunyan's creative talent is displayed even more in the character studies than in the painting of the background. Naturally the most detailed portrait is that of Christian, in whom the author has fused imaginatively the good and bad qualities which he has found and analysed in himself. Yet how flat this character is beside its model! How much richer is the real living figure captured in *Grace Abounding*! How much less strange are the battles fought by Christian against the monster Apollyon than the tinker's own demons and inner conflicts!

Bunyan has intentionally imposed a rather systematic order upon what is in real life tumult and chaos. He has apportioned out his experience and his being, giving a little of himself to several characters, allowing each one life and vitality, but not endowing any with all of his own complexity.

This is in no way surprising for Bunyan's intention was only to use intelligently the various traditions upon which he was drawing. His chosen literary form had its own requirements and limits, but within these limits the author has succeeded in giving life to a world whose bold contours give vigorous expression to the truth of his observation.

It is a world which has the variety of life itself, where homeliness mingles with grandeur and heightens it by contrast; a world where reality is peopled by the creatures of dreams, and where the marvellous is revealed to the creatures of earth; a world in which Bunyan believes because he sees it with intense clarity during the whole process of creation.

With what sure movements he leads us into this little universe! The first scene in the book affords a perfect example of this:

As I walk'd through the wilderness of this world, I lighted on a certain place, where was a den; and I laid me down in that place to sleep: and as I slept I dreamed, and behold I saw a man cloathed with rags standing in a certain place, with his face from his own house, a Book in his hand, and a great burden upon his back. I looked and saw him open the Book, and read therein; and as he read, he wept and trembled: and not being able any longer to contain, he brake out with a lamentable cry, saying, what shall I do?

Bunyan presents things in the bareness of their outlines; he does not clog his meaning by using adjectives. He multiplies the verbs, rejecting the imperfect form in favour of the aorist, and furnishes his sentences with short words, whose pure clear-sounding vowels are carried vigorously along by the firm compact consonants.

The ragged pilgrim, so forcefully portrayed at the very outset, throws his shadow over the whole book. The unity of the story is created around its symbolical hero.

Bunyan always links narrative and dialogue together very naturally. The dialogue is brisk, sprinkled with colloquialisms and racy proverbs:

His house is as empty of religion as the white of an egg is of savour . . . Will a man give a penny to fill his belly with hay? etc.

And always everywhere there is that simplicity which Coleridge considered necessary to works of imagination because only through simplicity can the reader enter fully into the fiction.

Bunyan commands a variety of tone. The familiar tone often becomes grave. The rather rugged phrasing of the dialogue follows a more musical and flowing passage of narrative. And if the good homely words used by the mystic pilgrims bind them to the earth, the biblical expressions and metaphors give to their horizon perspectives of infinity:

Now as they walked in this land, they had more rejoicing than in parts more remote from the Kingdom to which they were bound; and drawing near to the City they had yet a more perfect view thereof. It was builded of pearls and precious stones, also the street thereof was paved with gold, so that by reason of the natural glory of the City, and the reflections of the sunbeams upon it, Christian, with desire fell sick . . If you see my Beloved, tell him that I am sick of love.

Of course, the second part of *The Pilgrim's Progress* differs from the first in form as well as in content. The first book, being the story of a conversion, a man's spiritual biography, possesses a dramatic unity which the second lacks. What tension there is in the book resides in the life of the hero and is only a softened reflection of the vital tension of the author. The first book is a forerunner of those novels in which the passage of time reveals growth of character. The second book, on the other hand, heralds those in which the characters are static and remain unchanged in all circumstances. But both will stand the test of prolonged and detailed study better than many works which at first sight appear more brilliant.

The Pilgrim's Progress grows upon one as one becomes more familiar with it. It may disappoint at first, but it wins over every reader who gives it a friendly trial. It brings the riches of a strong personality, of thought, and of an ancient and deeply-rooted popular culture. It is both an individual and a collective work, and Mrs. Q. D. Leavis is right in saying: 'It is not fantastic to assert that it was the puritan culture as much as Bunyan that produced *The Pilgrim's Progress.*'

V

Grace Abounding and *The Pilgrim's Progress* reveal Bunyan at his best, but in order to measure his stature accurately, at least two more of his works must be considered: *The Life and Death of Mr. Badman* and *The Holy War*.

On the whole Bunyan specialists agree in admiring *The Pilgrim's Progress*, but as regards *Badman* they agree to differ —a point worth noting because it is significant: a book which provokes controversy is a live book. In a valuable article Mr. Maurice Hussey speaks unreservedly of the greatness of the work. Mr. Sharrock, in an excellent study, also expresses much admiration, though with a certain reserve. But both affirm the literary value of *Badman* rather than analyse it. They both, rightly, stress the historical interest of this work, but in so doing they defeat their own intention of taking it away from the student of history to offer it to a wider public. *Badman* certainly deserves more readers, precisely because social history is too rich a field to be turned into a private enclosure reserved for specialists only.

The work is at one and the same time a manual of personal, family and social behaviour, and a record of the habits of the middle class at the time of the Restoration. This record is not without pleasing sketches; but the central figure, who promised to overflow with life, for his rascality is of an extremely vigorous kind, is stifled by the didactic purpose of the author. He ceases to be a man and becomes a scarecrow, or, as Bunyan says in a moment of unconscious self-criticism, 'one massy body of sins', of all the vices in their very often picturesque seventeenth-century costumes.

Badman is not a person, he is an example intended to warn the reader by frightening him. He has his ancestor in the *exempla* of the mediaeval sermons and of various other books which Bunyan was fond of, such as Samuel Clark's *A Mirrour and Looking-Glass for Both Saints and Sinners*.

Since Badman is Christian's counterpart, it is permissible to compare them. Christian is a truly symbolic personage, that is to say he is rich in potentialities. He is not squeezed into an allegorical garment which paralyses him. Badman has none of the suppleness and diversity which are qualities of the true symbol as they are qualities of life. He does not come before us as a creature of flesh and blood in whom we can believe; nor has he the power of one of those great conventional literary creations which in spite of everything are endued with something of the mystery of life.

Every work of art possesses an internal coherence, every great work of literature is a universe with its own atmosphere, its own being which belong so completely to it that they appear unreal, or ridiculous, or lifeless outside of it. *Badman* does not fulfil either of these criteria. It is the biography, tortuous yet void of surprise, of a model scoundrel who becomes more and more wicked in obedience to a determinism as pitiless as Calvin's predestination. Nowhere do I feel the author's creative imagination at work, either in the portrait of the principal figure or in the pictures of social life.

It is usual to praise the book's realism, but is there any value in the realism which is no more than a reproduction of ordinary life? True realism is a creation, not a copy. Bunyan has failed to re-create the society which he has observed; all he has done is to provide laborious illustrations of its customs and its spirit.

These illustrations are nevertheless always interesting. The observation is precise, picturesque, plentiful. The strokes of the drawing are rather thick, rather heavy, but they are not blurred. Even if Bunyan has lost the creative joy which bore him along on an irresistible wave in the wake of the heavenly pilgrims, he has lost none of his force and none of his good workmanship.

True, the dialogue is sometimes wearisome. We hear the Bunyan of the meeting-house instead of the Bunyan of Parnassus. But at its best the sentence is sinewy, the vocabulary keeps its concrete and evocative solidity. And the student of literary history will find in *Badman* a notable landmark on the way leading to the flowering of the novel in the eighteenth century.

Like *Badman*, *The Holy War* is a work 'obtained' rather than a work 'given', but nowhere are Bunyan's subtlety and the extent of his knowledge more marked.

It is another allegory, in which it may be said that, among other things, Bunyan proposes to justify the ways of God to Man, according to his own ideas. The work has its epic moments, such as the account of the fall of the angels and their attack upon the human soul. But the author is not content with that. He returns to the story of his conversion and of his inner conflicts, enlarging his scope still further. After the journey of Christian, we now have the struggle of an entire city. Moreover, secondary themes are associated with the main theme of conversion. A political and social theme based upon contemporary events runs through the book; and a sectarian theme also appears occasionally, connected with belief in the millennium, or in what was then called the Fifth Monarchy.

For these themes to have been fused into a coherent story, they would have had to respond to one another like the melodies of a fugue, to have been represented by the same symbols, and to have mingled without either losing themselves or conflicting. But no amount of skill in literary counterpoint could have succeeded or could ever succeed in harmonizing such discordant strains.

The Holy War provides an interesting example of the failure of a man who goes against his own genius. Bunyan, a spontaneous writer, is never more felicitous than when he is driven on by his passion and the fervour of his inspiration, and lets his pen run away with him; yet he spent two years in contriving and arranging the meanings of his allegory according to architectural plans which, despite their admirable boldness, are totally lacking in harmony and clarity.

The Holy War is a failure, but it is the superb failure of a great ambition, the failure of a vigorous and courageous intelligence.

VI

Bunyan's strong personality unites and harmonizes opposing qualities. A manual worker, he was essentially an intellectual in the only sense the word ought to bear: he was not only a man who loved books (Bunyan may have read little but he thought deeply about what he read), but a man whose thought directed and governed his life.

But he was an intellectual who became a writer less from a taste for writing—however pronounced that taste may have been—than from a sense of duty and the need to act;

for with him, writing was primarily a form of action. And this action found its meaning and its spring in his religious and moral fervour, as his great allegories found their inspiration in his dreams and mystical visions.

Though Bunyan felt the potency of words, he never yielded to it without disciplining his pleasure and submitting it to a purpose. Without the genius which so often raised him above commonplace didacticism, he would only have been an energetic preacher, gifted with great verbal facility. Of course a work of art teaches also, but it is by offering a vision of order and not by enunciating precepts.

Having suffered, struggled, meditated, in short having lived fully, Bunyan could pour into his work the riches of an authentic existence: his difficult growth, the conflicts of his divided mind, the unifying force of a faith deepened by action, then the fruit of it all—gravity and dignity without inflexibility, wider human understanding, warm sympathy towards people and a tranquil attitude towards things.

As he said himself almost in so many words, the solemn music of the bass gave way to the joyful chords of the high notes. To achieve maturity, to conquer his soul, was for him to reach the clear harmonies of the trumpet and the harp:

The first string that the musician usually touches is the base, when he intends to put all in tune. God also plays upon this string first . . . (but) in the Book of the Revelations, the Saved are compared to a company of Musicians that play upon their trumpets and harps, and sing their songs before the Throne.

Bunyan presents at one and the same time the true aspect of Puritanism—which is not the fanaticism with which it has often been wilfully confused—and the spectacle of a type of humanity which transcends the doctrine and the age that formed it.

His work has gained in power and in profundity from having been born in hours of oppression and sorrow rather than in the exaltation of the shortlived triumph of Puritanism. This late birth brought it the twofold benefit of the author's broader human experience and of a closer agreement with the nation as a whole. Puritanism would hardly have understood its own nature so well if it had sought to express itself in the fever of action. In its time for remembering, it was fortunate in finding an artist for whom memory was the soul of thought.

JOHN BUNYAN
A Select Bibliography
(Place of publication London, unless stated otherwise)

Bibliography:

LIFE OF JOHN BUNYAN, by E. Venables (1888)
—contains a bibliography by J. P. Anderson of Bunyan's works, and of critical and biographical studies.

THE PILGRIM'S PROGRESS, ed. J. B. Wharey. Oxford (1928). Second edition, revised by R. Sharrock, Oxford, 1960
—contains a bibliography of the first editions of *The Pilgrim's Progress*.

BIBLIOGRAPHY OF THE WORKS OF JOHN BUNYAN, by F. M. Harrison (Suppl. to the *Bibliogr. Soc. Trans.*, 6). Oxford (1932).

CATALOGUE OF THE JOHN BUNYAN LIBRARY, by F. M. Harrison (Frank Mott Harrison Collection, Bedford Public Library). Bedford (1938).

A HANDLIST OF EDITIONS OF THE FIRST PART OF THE PILGRIM'S PROGRESS, by F. M. Harrison. Hove (1941).

'Notes on the early editions of *Grace Abounding*', by F. M. Harrison. *Baptist Quarterly*, vol. XI (1943).

Collected Works:

THE WORKS OF THAT EMINENT SERVANT OF CHRIST, MR. JOHN BUNYAN . . . Together with a large alphabetical table (by C. Doe). With a prefatory epistle by E. Chandler and J. Wilson, 1 vol. fol. (1692).

THE SECOND EDITION (with additions), 2 vols. (1736).

THE THIRD EDITION (with new additions, and a preface by the Rev. G. Whitefield), 2 vols. (1767-8).

THE WORKS OF JOHN BUNYAN, with an introduction to each treatise, notes, and a sketch of his life, times, and contemporaries, ed. G. Offor, 3 vols. Glasgow (1853). Reprinted, London, 1862.

THE ENTIRE WORKS OF JOHN BUNYAN, edited with original introductions, notes, and a memoir of the author, by H. Stebbing, 4 vols. (1859-60).

Selected Works:

SELECTIONS FROM BUNYAN, ed. W. T. Williams and G. H. Vallins (1927).

GOD'S KNOTTY LOG. Selected Writings of John Bunyan, edited and introduced by H. A. Talon. New York (1961).

Separate Works:

SOME GOSPEL-TRUTHS OPENED (1656).

A VINDICATION OF SOME GOSPEL-TRUTHS (1657).

A FEW SIGNS FROM HELL (1658).

THE DOCTRINE OF THE LAW AND GRACE UNFOLDED (1659).

PROFITABLE MEDITATIONS (1661).

CHRISTIAN BEHAVIOUR (1663).

I WILL PRAY WITH THE SPIRIT (1663).

A MAPP OF SALVATION AND DAMNATION (c. 1664).

THE HOLY CITY (1665).

THE RESURRECTION OF THE DEAD (1665).

GRACE ABOUNDING (1666).

A CONFESSION OF MY FAITH (1672).

A DEFENCE OF THE DOCTRINE OF JUSTIFICATION (1672).

DIFFERENCES . . . ABOUT WATER BAPTISM (1673).

PEACEABLE PRINCIPLES AND TRUE (1674).

REPROBATION ASSERTED (c. 1674).

[John Brown denies Bunyan's authorship of the work.]

INSTRUCTION FOR THE IGNORANT (1675).

LIGHT FOR THEM THAT SIT IN DARKNESS (1675).

SAVED BY GRACE (1676).

THE STRAIT GATE (1676).

COME AND WELCOME, TO JESUS CHRIST (1678).

THE PILGRIM'S PROGRESS, Part I (1678).

A TREATISE OF THE FEAR OF GOD (1679).

THE LIFE AND DEATH OF MR. BADMAN (1680).

THE HOLY WAR (1682).

A CASE OF CONSCIENCE RESOLVED (1683).

THE GREATNESS OF THE SOUL (1683).

ONE THING IS NEEDFUL (1683).

A CAUTION TO STIR UP (1684).

A HOLY LIFE (1684).

THE PILGRIM'S PROGRESS, Part II (1684).

SEASONABLE COUNSEL (1684).

A DISCOURSE UPON THE PHARISEE AND THE PUBLICAN (1685).

QUESTIONS ABOUT THE SEVENTH-DAY SABBATH (1685).

A BOOK FOR BOYS AND GIRLS (1686).

THE ADVOCATESHIP OF JESUS CHRIST (1688).

THE BARREN FIG TREE (1688).

A DISCOURSE . . . OF THE HOUSE OF GOD (1688).

GOOD NEWS FOR THE VILEST OF MEN (1688).
   [Title altered to *The Jerusalem Sinner Saved; or Good News for etc.*, in second edition, 1689].

SOLOMON'S TEMPLE SPIRITUALIZED (1688).

THE WATER OF LIFE (1688).

THE ACCEPTABLE SACRIFICE (1689).

Posthumous:

OF ANTICHRIST AND HIS RUIN, Doe's folio (1692).

CHRIST A COMPLETE SAVIOUR, ibid.

A CHRISTIAN DIALOGUE (date and all other particulars unknown).

A NEW AND USEFUL CONCORDANCE. (No copy known. Doe says he bought the MS. in 1691.)

THE DESIRES OF THE RIGHTEOUS GRANTED (1692).

AN ÆXPOSITION OF GENESIS (1692).

THE HEAVENLY FOOTMAN [date unknown, but the book was begun before *The Pilgrim's Progress*]. Printed for Charles Doe (1698).

OF THE HOUSE OF THE FOREST OF LEBANON (1692).

ISRAEL'S HOPE ENCOURAGED (1692).

OF JUSTIFICATION BY IMPUTED RIGHTEOUSNESS (1692).

OF THE LAW AND A CHRISTIAN (Collected Works, Vol. I) (1736).

PAUL'S DEPARTURE AND CROWN (1692).

A RELATION OF THE IMPRISONMENT OF MR. JOHN BUNYAN (only ed., 1765).

THE SAINT'S KNOWLEDGE OF CHRIST'S LOVE (1692).

THE SAINT'S PRIVILEDGE AND PROFIT (1692).

MR. JOHN BUNYAN'S LAST SERMON (1689).

OF THE TRINITY AND A CHRISTIAN (Collected Works, Vol. I) (1736).

Facsimile and Annotated Editions (A Selection):

THE PILGRIM'S PROGRESS as originally published, being a facsimile reproduction of the first edition. 1875, 1877, 1895, 1930.

THE PILGRIM'S PROGRESS, printed from the first edition, with notices of all the subsequent additions made by the author himself, edited for the Hansard Knollys Society, with an introduction by G. Offor (1847).

THE PILGRIM'S PROGRESS, edited with introduction and notes by the Rev. J. Brown (1887).

THE PILGRIM'S PROGRESS, ed. J. B. Wharey. Oxford (1928). Second edition, revised by R. Sharrock, Oxford, 1960.

THE PILGRIM'S PROGRESS, GRACE ABOUNDING, and A RELATION OF BUNYAN'S IMPRISONMENT, edited with introduction and notes by E. Venables. Oxford (1879). Second edition, revised by M. Peacock, 1900.

THE PILGRIM'S PROGRESS and THE LIFE AND DEATH OF MR. BADMAN, with an introduction by G. B. Harrison (1928).

GRACE ABOUNDING and THE PILGRIM'S PROGRESS, ed. J. Brown (1907).

GRACE ABOUNDING and THE LIFE AND DEATH OF MR. BADMAN, ed. G. B. Harrison (1928).

GRACE ABOUNDING, ed. R. Sharrock. Oxford (1962).

THE LIFE AND DEATH OF MR. BADMAN and THE HOLY WAR, ed. J. Brown (1905).

THE LIFE AND DEATH OF MR. BADMAN, with an introduction by B. Dobrée (1929)
—in the World's Classics edition.

THE HOLY WAR, ed. J. Brown (1887).

THE HOLY WAR and THE HEAVENLY FOOTMAN, with an introduction and notes by M. Peacock. Oxford (1892).

Some Critical and Biographical Studies:

THE PILGRIM'S PROGRESS, ed. R. Southey (1830)
—contains an introduction by Southey. Reprinted in his *Select Biographies*, 1844.

CRITICAL AND HISTORICAL ESSAYS, by T. B. Macaulay, 3 vols. (1843)
—vol. I contains an essay 'John Bunyan'. Published separately, Cambridge, 1898, and Oxford, 1914.

STUDIES IN THE ENGLISH OF BUNYAN, by J. B. Grier. Philadelphia (1872).

JOHN BUNYAN, by J. A. Froude (1880).

JOHN BUNYAN, HIS LIFE, TIMES AND WORK, by J. Brown (1885). Revised by F. M. Harrison, 1928.

A STUDY OF THE SOURCES OF BUNYAN'S ALLEGORIES, by J. B. Wharey.
   Baltimore (1904)
—with special reference to Deguileville's *Pilgrimage of Man*.

JOHN BUNYAN, by W. H. White ['Mark Rutherford'] (1905).

DRAMATIC OPINIONS AND ESSAYS, by G. B. Shaw (1907)
—contains an essay on Bunyan.

JOHN BUNYAN, by C. H. Firth (English Association leaflet, No. 19)
   (1911)
—reprinted in his *Essays Historical and Literary*, Oxford, 1938.

JOHN BUNYAN, by G. O. Griffith (1927).

JOHN BUNYAN, A STUDY IN PERSONALITY, by G. B. Harrison (1928).

JOHN BUNYAN, MECHANICK PREACHER, by W. Y. Tindall. New York
   (1934).

BUNYAN CALLING: A VOICE FROM THE SEVENTEENTH CENTURY, by M. P.
   Willcocks (1943).

'Bunyan and the English Emblem Writers', by R. Sharrock. *Review of
   English Studies*, April 1945.

'Spiritual Autobiography in *The Pilgrim's Progress*', by R. Sharrock.
   Review of English Studies, April 1948.

'Bunyan's Mr. Ignorance', by M. Hussey. *Modern Language Review*,
   October 1949.

'Bunyan's *The Life and Death of Mr. Badman*', by M. Hussey.
   Congregational Quarterly, November 1950.

JOHN BUNYAN, THE MAN AND HIS WORKS, by H. A. Talon (1951).

THE COMMON PURSUIT, by F. R. Leavis (1952)
—contains an essay 'Bunyan Through Modern Eyes'.

THE ENGLISH NOVEL. FORM AND FUNCTION, by D. Van Ghent. New
   York (1953)
—contains a chapter 'On *The Pilgrim's Progress*'.

JOHN BUNYAN, by R. Sharrock (1954).

'Bunyan and the Puritan Culture', by L. D. Lerner. *Cambridge Journal*,
   January 1954.

'Allégorie et Réalisme dans *The Pilgrim's Progress*', par J. Blondel.
   Archives des Lettres Modernes. Paris, 1959.

'Bunyan's *Pilgrim's Progress:* Die Kalvinistische Heilsgewissheit und die
   form des Romans', von W. Iser. In *Festschrift für Walther Bulst*.
   Heidelberg, 1960.

'Space and the Hero in *The Pilgrim's Progress*', par H. A. Talon. *Etudes anglaises*, avril-juin, 1961.

'Bunyan's Ignorance and the Flatterer: A Study in the Literary Art of Damnation', by J. F. Forrest. *Studies in Philology*, January 1963.

'Mercy with her Mirror', by J. F. Forrest. *Philological Quarterly*, January 1963.

BUNYAN ALS KÜNSTLER. STILKRITISCHE STUDIEN ZU SEINEM HAUPTWERK THE PILGRIM'S PROGRESS, von B. Haferkamp. Tübingen, 1963.

WRITERS AND THEIR WORK

General Editor: BONAMY DOBRÉE

The first 55 issues in the Series appeared under the General Editorship of T. O. BEACHCROFT

Sixteenth Century and Earlier:

FRANCIS BACON: J. Max Patrick
CHAUCER: Nevill Coghill
ENGLISH BIBLE: Donald Coggan
ENGLISH MARITIME WRITING:
    Hakluyt to Cook: Oliver Warner
MALORY: M. C. Bradbrook
MARLOWE: Philip Henderson
SIDNEY: Kenneth Muir
SKELTON: Peter Green
SPENSER: Rosemary Freeman
WYATT: Sergio Baldi

Seventeenth Century:

SIR THOMAS BROWNE: Peter Green
BUNYAN: Henri Talon
CAVALIER POETS: Robin Skelton
CONGREVE: Bonamy Dobrée
DONNE: F. Kermode
DRYDEN: Bonamy Dobrée
ENGLISH DIARISTS: Margaret Willy
ENGLISH SERMONS: Arthur Pollard
GEORGE HERBERT: T. S. Eliot
HERRICK: John Press
HOBBES: T. E. Jessop
BEN JONSON: J. B. Bamborough
LOCKE: Maurice Cranston
ANDREW MARVELL: John Press
MILTON: E. M. W. Tillyard
SHAKESPEARE: C. J. Sisson
SHAKESPEARE:
  CHRONICLES: Clifford Leech
  EARLY COMEDIES: Derek Traversi
  FINAL PLAYS: F. Kermode
  HISTORIES: L. C. Knights
  LATE COMEDIES: G. K. Hunter
  THE POEMS: F. T. Prince
  PROBLEM PLAYS: Peter Ure
  ROMAN PLAYS: T. J. B. Spencer
  GREAT TRAGEDIES: Kenneth Muir
THREE METAPHYSICAL POETS:
    Margaret Willy
IZAAK WALTON: Margaret Bottrall

Eighteenth Century:

BERKELEY: T. E. Jessop

BLAKE: Kathleen Raine
BOSWELL: P. A. W. Collins
BURKE: T. E. Utley
BURNS: David Daiches
COWPER: N. Nicholson
CRABBE: R. L. Brett
DEFOE: J. R. Sutherland
ENGLISH HYMNS: Arthur Pollard
FIELDING: John Butt
GIBBON: C. V. Wedgwood
GOLDSMITH: A. Norman Jeffares
GRAY: R. W. Ketton-Cremer
JOHNSON: S. C. Roberts
POPE: Ian Jack
RICHARDSON: R. F. Brissenden
SHERIDAN: W. A. Darlington
CHRISTOPHER SMART:
    Geoffrey Grigson
SMOLLETT: Laurence Brander
STEELE AND ADDISON:
    A. R. Humphreys
STERNE: D. W. Jefferson
SWIFT: J. Middleton Murry
HORACE WALPOLE: Hugh Honour

Nineteenth Century:

MATTHEW ARNOLD: Kenneth Allott
JANE AUSTEN: S. Townsend Warner
BAGEHOT: N. St. John-Stevas
THE BRONTE SISTERS: P. Bentley
BROWNING: John Bryson
SAMUEL BUTLER: G. D. H. Cole
BYRON: Herbert Read
CARLYLE: David Gascoyne
LEWIS CARROLL: Derek Hudson
CLOUGH: I. Armstrong
COLERIDGE: Kathleen Raine
DE QUINCEY: Hugh Sykes Davies
DICKENS: K. J. Fielding
DISRAELI: Paul Bloomfield
GEORGE ELIOT: Lettice Cooper
ENGLISH TRAVELLERS IN THE NEAR
  EAST: Robin Fedden
FITZGERALD: Joanna Richardson
MRS. GASKELL: Miriam Allott
GISSING: A. C. Ward

THOMAS HARDY: R. A. Scott-James
HAZLITT: J. B. Priestley
HOOD: Laurence Brander
G. M. HOPKINS: Geoffrey Grigson
T. H. HUXLEY: William Irvine
KEATS: Edmund Blunden
LAMB: Edmund Blunden
LANDOR: G. Rostrevor Hamilton
MACAULAY: G. R. Potter
MEREDITH: Phyllis Bartlett
JOHN STUART MILL: M. Cranston
WILLIAM MORRIS: P. Henderson
NEWMAN: J. M. Cameron
PATER: Iain Fletcher
PEACOCK: J. I. M. Stewart
ROSSETTI: Oswald Doughty
RUSKIN: Peter Quennell
SIR WALTER SCOTT: Ian Jack
SHELLEY: Stephen Spender
R. L. STEVENSON: G. B. Stern
SWINBURNE: H. J. C. Grierson
TENNYSON: F. L. Lucas
THACKERAY: Laurence Brander
FRANCIS THOMPSON: P. Butter
TROLLOPE: Hugh Sykes Davies
OSCAR WILDE: James Laver
WORDSWORTH: Helen Darbishire

Twentieth Century:

W. H. AUDEN: Richard Hoggart
HILAIRE BELLOC: Renée Haynes
ARNOLD BENNETT: F. Swinnerton
EDMUND BLUNDEN: Alec M. Hardie
ELIZABETH BOWEN: Jocelyn Brooke
ROBERT BRIDGES: J. Sparrow
ROY CAMPBELL: David Wright
JOYCE CARY: Walter Allen
G. K. CHESTERTON: C. Hollis
WINSTON CHURCHILL: John Connell
R.G. COLLINGWOOD: E.W.F. Tomlin
I. COMPTON-BURNETT:
          Pamela Hansford Johnson
JOSEPH CONRAD: Oliver Warner
WALTER DE LA MARE: K. Hopkins
THE DETECTIVE STORY IN
          BRITAIN: Julian Symons
NORMAN DOUGLAS: Ian Greenlees
T. S. ELIOT: M. C. Bradbrook
FIRBANK & BETJEMAN: J. Brooke

FORD MADOX FORD: Kenneth Young
E. M. FORSTER: Rex Warner
CHRISTOPHER FRY: Derek Stanford
JOHN GALSWORTHY: R. H. Mottram
ROBERT GRAVES: M. Seymour Smith
GRAHAM GREENE: Francis Wyndham
L. P. HARTLEY & ANTHONY POWELL:
          P. Bloomfield and B. Bergonzi
A. E. HOUSMAN: Ian Scott-Kilvert
ALDOUS HUXLEY: Jocelyn Brooke
HENRY JAMES: Michael Swan
JAMES JOYCE: J. I. M. Stewart
KIPLING: Bonamy Dobrée
D. H. LAWRENCE: Kenneth Young
C. DAY LEWIS: Clifford Dyment
WYNDHAM LEWIS: E. W. F. Tomlin
KATHERINE MANSFIELD: Ian Gordon
JOHN MASEFIELD: L. A. G. Strong
SOMERSET MAUGHAM: J. Brophy
EDWIN MUIR: J. C. Hall
J. MIDDLETON MURRY: Philip Mairet
GEORGE ORWELL: Tom Hopkinson
POETS OF 1939-45 WAR:
          R. N. Currey
POWYS BROTHERS: R. C. Churchill
J. B. PRIESTLEY: Ivor Brown
HERBERT READ: Francis Berry
BERTRAND RUSSELL: Alan Dorward
BERNARD SHAW: A. C. Ward
EDITH SITWELL: John Lehmann
OSBERT SITWELL: Roger Fulford
C. P. SNOW: William Cooper
STRACHEY: R. A. Scott-James
SYNGE & LADY GREGORY:
          E. Coxhead
DYLAN THOMAS: G. S. Fraser
EDWARD THOMAS: Vernon Scannell
G. M. TREVELYAN: J. H. Plumb
WAR POETS: 1914-18:
          Edmund Blunden
EVELYN WAUGH: Christopher Hollis
H. G. WELLS: Montgomery Belgion
CHARLES WILLIAMS:
          John Heath-Stubbs
VIRGINIA WOOLF: Bernard Blackstone
W. B. YEATS: G. S. Fraser
ANDREW YOUNG & R. S. THOMAS:
          L. Clark and R. G. Thomas